# Spotted Dick, Toad-in-the-Hole and Bubble and Squeak

## Recipes for Classic English Dishes

## Keith Pepperell

## DEDICATION

To my hungry spawn Jack, Alexandra, and Lydia all of whom like British nosh

# ACKNOWLEDGMENTS

Lady Joan Pepperell

Sir Francis Pepperell

Lady Estima Davenport

Professor Muriel Dinwiddy

Annie Mole

Aterux

British Ministry of Education

Jeremy Keith (Welsh Rarebit Image)

Judgeej (Faggots Image)

Ewan Monroe (Christmas Lunch)

Krista - Goodies First (Stargazy Pie)

Jean-Christophe Benoist - Constantine

Secretlondon (Jellied Eels Image)

Natus (Scotch Eggs Image)

Theorb (The Full English

E4tjc - Full English Image)

## 1 BRITISH NOSH

The Brits like their cuisine, fare, grits, eatables, comestibles, snacks, nutriment, meals, bites, fodder, cheer, chow, eats, goodies, cookery, mess, menus, viands, nourishment, slop, victuals and vittles.

Americans (who eat grits, corn dogs, green bean casseroles, and American non-dairy processed cheese slices) believe there is no British cuisine and would consider most of the lovely dishes described herein as entirely fictitious. Of course they also patriotically hail from a nation that has never let facts get in the way of anything.

This little volume aspires to provide some history together with some splendid and easy recipes most beloved by the limeys.

These have largely been kept secret even though rings of ruthless German spies attempted to discover the dishes that both fueled and sustained British spirit during World War II.

They were not successful and many were caught with their fingers in both savory and fruit pies.

The secrets of Toad-in-the-Hole, Faggots, Spotted Dick, Haggis, Welsh

Rarebit, Bubble and Squeak, Stargazy Pie, Scotch Eggs, Jam Roly-Poly, Bangers and Mash, Jellied Eels, The Full English, and a Traditional Christmas Dinner will be revealed herein.

The author has had plastic surgery and a total identity change to avoid both suspicion and capture by legions of British cooks who want to keep these recipes to themselves and are out for his blood.

Even though these dishes may seem a little odd, they are certainly not quite as odd as Casa Marzu (maggot ridden decomposed sheep milk cheese), Pacha (boiled sheep's head), Escamoles (eggs of the venomous Liometopum ant), Balut (the boiled alive and partially incubated crunchy duck fetuses) Lutefish (fermented cod the odor of which is strong enough to remove cataracts) Baby White Mice (fermented in rice wine,) and Bird's Nest Soup (made from the roost of the White-Nest Swiftlet).

A tasty dish of Balut by Aterux

Americans seem particularly keen to announce loudly and somewhat boorishly that there is no such thing as British cuisine, Brits drink their beer warm, and cricket is dull.

Enough said!

## 2 TOAD-IN-THE-HOLE

## (Naughty sausages baked in a batter pudding with sherry and onion gravy)

Annie Mole's glorious Toad-in-the-Hole

with delightfully unctuous onion gravy

For a little over two hundred years the Brits have enjoyed this enigmatically named dish. It is most delightful when served with a sherry infused onion gravy and a dollop or two of Coleman's marvelous English mustard.

Like so many other dishes, there is little agreement as to the origins of the name.

Some have claimed the name reflects (i) the appearance of the head of a toad poking out of its hiding place, (ii) a toad poking its head out of the cup on a golf green.

The author once came across a small vole that had tumbled into a cup. It was carefully removed and taken to a safe place.

Later, following some lively debate and a fist fight, the Rules Committee of the Royal and Ancient concluded a two shot penalty was too harsh and that the vole should have been dropped no more two club lengths from the cup under Rule 926 (b) (iii) Vole under Repair without penalty.

What is known is that the earliest references appear in the eighteenth century when 'batter puddings' (see post) became popular. There is a recorded example of an 'in the hole' dish when a recipe for pigeon in the hole appears in  Hannah Glasse's *The Art of Cookery, Made Plain and Easy - That Far Exceeds Anything Yet Published (1747)*. *Ms. Glasse* seems to have started a trend when the plentiful pigeon was replaced by the noble banger (see post).

There appear to be other batter pudding based dishes with sausages (toad) as in when the Georgian diarist and merchant Thomas Turner records in 1757 "sausages baked in a batter pudding".

It also seems clear that the working classes were most likely to eat toad-in-the-hole since sausages were comparatively inexpensive and to eat more expensive cuts of meat in a batter pudding was considered rather vulgar. Prissy novelist Fanny Burney mentions disapprovingly the trend for "putting a noble sirloin of beef into a poor paltry batter-pudding".

Certainly the author enjoyed many

spectacular toads from his dear old mum's kitchen.

Lady Joan's batter pudding was remarkable for both the golden crust's gravity defying rise and its spectacular lightness.

She obtained her bangers from Mr. Finning the Butcher down in the village whose sawdust covered floor and massive butcher's block the author recalls with great affection.

Game birds hung invitingly from a great rack above the counter and naughty plum pork sausages beckoned invitingly beneath the glass counter top.

On the village green nearby the occasional Mallard Duck would peer uncomfortably in Mr. Finning's general direction. Mr. Finning would never give up his herb infused sausage recipe even to the mysterious and inquisitive Miss Vollweiller who was later unmasked as a German spy.

It seems she had offered certain 'carnal favors' to plump and otherwise unremarkable butcher's boy Sidney Widgeon who stayed remarkably stum even while she was vigorously pumping up the tire of his iconic delivery tricycle with the wicker basket on the front.

The recipe for herb infused sausages (see *post*) comes from the little known Suffolk Village of Woollard End where the elderly Home Guard kept the recipe out of the hands of German paratroopers in 1943 after a plucky nocturnal counter-attack using only thatching tools, baked potatoes, and pitchforks.

The term 'banger' was used immediately after World War I even though its origins are otherwise shrouded in mystery.

One account involved the adding of water to sausages to 'fill them out a bit' during hard times.

During cooking they would splutter and occasionally violently explode.

A Miss Ophelia Merkin of Henley-on-Thames, who was of a particularly nervous disposition, once passed out when a sausage exploded in a nearby kitchen.

As she slid indecorously to the floor she recalled former unpleasant images of German flying bombs over London in the blitz. She was revived with several stiff ports and lemon.

A vigorous pricking of the sausage skins with a sharp fork will serve to prevent explosions and provide a pleasant high pitched flatulent sound during cooking

## Ingredients for Herby Sausages

12 ounces nice lean pork preferably organic, minced

4 ounces lovely plump pork belly, minced

2 ounces fresh white breadcrumbs

1 white onion, peeled & grated

1/2 lemon rind (zesty) finely grated

A pinch of a little nutmeg finely grated

1 teaspoon chopped curly parsley

2 teaspoons of fresh herbs (sage, thyme and marjoram) - at a pinch dried herbs will work but only one teaspoon

1 teaspoon freshly ground black or white pepper

Kosher (or nun blessed) salt to taste

2 nice brown free range eggs vigorously beaten

1/2 tablespoon all-purpose flour

1 egg white, only

1 ounce best butter

1 tablespoon light vegetable oil

## Preparation Method

1. Combine all the lovely meats with the fresh breadcrumbs, grated white onion, lemon rind, nutmeg, parsley, fresh or dried herbs, pepper & salt. Mix well. It is better (and far more

pleasing) to mix this together with
your delightfully manicured spotless
hands.


2. Bind with the 2 beaten eggs &
mix well again.
3.   Chill the sausage mixture in the
fridge — it will easier to handle when
it is slightly firmer. You can also
use the mixture for stuffing a bird at
this stage too. When you are ready to
cook the sausages form the mixture
into sausage shapes — using a little
flour to help you.
4.   Dip the sausages into the beaten
egg white and then dust lightly with
the flour and set aside until you are
ready to use them.
5.   Heat the oil and butter together
in a large frying pan (deep sided is
better since they like to spit a

little) and cook the sausages for about 10-15 minutes over a medium heat.

6.   Turn them regularly to ensure they brown evenly. This browning makes them more pleasing in appearance even though they will be cooked further in the batter. Reserve 6 of them.

## Ingredients for Batter Pudding (Yorkshire) with the Sausages Nestling Naughtily Therein

2 lovely brown free-range eggs

*4½ oz plain flower*

5fl oz milk mixed with 150ml cold water

1 level tablespoon of grain mustard

Maldon salt and freshly ground white pepper

6 naughtily plump, herby pork sausage - nothing foreign of course,

particularly anything faintly American or French.

3½ oz thinly sliced rashers of streaky bacon

3 tablespoons of pork dripping

**Preparation Method**

1. Whisk together the eggs, flour, milk, mustard and seasoning, give a vigorous thrashing to remove any annoying little lumps of flour. The consistency should now be about that of ordinary double cream, but no thinner.

2. Let the lovely mixture rest for 15 minutes preferable in a cool place or refrigerator while you drink two beers.

3.  Preheat the oven to 425F and then

carefully wrap the sausage meat in a piece of the nice streaky bacon without throttling it.

4. Place the pork dripping in a roasting tin and leave it in the oven until it is slightly smoking.

5. Pour in the batter, it will sizzle while basking happily in the hot fat - then arrange the sausages in the batter.

6. Transfer the tin back into the oven and bake for 25-30 minutes until puffed and golden. Serve wonderfully moistened with lashings of caramelised red onion and sherry gravy and a great dollop of magnificent Coleman's English mustard.

## Ingredients for Glorious Red Onion and Sherry Gravy

This lovely gravy can be liberally splashed over toad-in the-hole to give it a tasty moistening or is glorious when applied to bubble and squeak (see post), grilled calves liver, or mashed potatoes for bangers and mash(see post) etc.

A big dollop of butter

Two large red onions, peeled and very thinly sliced

A level tablespoon of flour

A big dollop of butter

Two large red onions, peeled and very thinly sliced

A level tablespoon of flour

1/3 of a cup of cooking sherry

1 and a half cups of stock

A dribble of Worcestershire sauce

## Preparation method

1. Melt the butter in a heavy pan, throw in the thinly sliced onions and cook gently over a low heat till sexily reddish gold and soft. Be careful not to burn them. Even the French won't eat them burnt.

2. Continue cooking, covered with a lid until the onions are truly reddish brown and soft enough to squish between your fingers (take care to let them cool before checking for degree of squish.)

3. Stir into the nicely reposing onions a level heaped tablespoon of flour and cook slowly for a few minutes until all is lightly browned.

4. Pour in the liquids. Season with salt and pepper and Worcestershire sauce and bring to a slow boil.

5. Turn down the heat so that the gravy bubbles nicely and gently and leave for about fifteen minutes, stirring from time to time. Drink a beer or two while you wait.

6. Pour gently into your best porcelain gravy boat (especially 18$^{th}$ century Worcester or Bow) and use scrumptiously sloshing over your toad-in-the-hole as required.

The Yorkshire pudding base can always be prepared without the naughty herby sausages and enjoyed as a splendid accompaniment to a typical British Sunday lunch — often with roast beef.

Lady Ophelia Mynnge out to taste a
fine Spotted Dick in 1942

### 3 SPOTTED DICK WITH BIRD'S CUSTARD

The origins of the name of this
delightfully naughtily unctuous
steamed, suety, current filled,
oozing, pudding, beloved of the
English is shrouded in mystery.

The earliest the earliest recorded

reference is in Alexis Soyer's The *Modern Housewife or Menagerie* (1849) where there is a recipe for 'Plum Bolster, or Spotted Dick'.

Spotted dick is a lovely British pudding made from suet, or mutton fat. The suet is mixed with other ingredients, creates a dough, the dough is then either steamed or boiled and is served with a custard of which bird's is the best.

The word 'dick' has several uses including; an apron, a dictionary, a policeman, a riding whip or crop, and a gentleman's person.

The word "could also be "a corruption of the last syllable of pudding, a corruption of 'dough', or a reference to the German *dick*, meaning thick or viscous".

During the seventeenth and eighteenth century suet based puddings became popular since they could also be cooked with a glorious meat and gravy filling as in steak and kidney pudding. The basic suet pudding was infinitely variable both sweet and savory. The cooking method involves using a 'pudding cloth' or cheesecloth.

Whatever the origins of the name, the 'spotted' part refers to the currents plumply loitering on the surface of the pudding.

## Ingredients

250g self-raising flour

Pinch of Kosher or nun-blessed salt

125g best shredded suet

180g plump naughty currants

80g caster sugar

Finely grated zest 1 lemon

Finely grated zest 1 small orange

150ml whole milk, plus 2-3 tablespoons
for later

**Preparation method**

1. Put the flour and salt in a bowl.
Add the suet, currants, sugar, lemon
and orange zest.

2. Pour in 150ml milk and mix to a
wonderfully firm but moist dough,
adding a little extra milk if
necessary.

3. Shape into a wonderfully plump roll
about 20cm long. Place on a large

rectangle of baking parchment. Wrap loosely to allow for the pudding to rise and tie the ends with string like a Christmas cracker.

4. Place a steamer over a large pan of boiling water, add the pudding to the steamer, cover and steam for 1 1/2 hours. Take special care to top up the pan with water from time to time.

5. Remove from the steamer and allow cooling slightly before ceremonially unwrapping accompanied by an old 78 scratchy recording of the National Anthem.
Bow one's head.
Serve sliced with a nice big boat of splendidly creamy Bird's custard. The recipe for making the custard will be on the tin but use whipping cream or

half-an-half for better results. Don't buy it pre-made. The latter can be used for wallpapering or to keeping wolves from your property.

## 4 BUBBLE AND SQUEAK

Americans are not at all comfortable with food that is (i) not served on a stick (ii) not featuring non-dairy processed American cheese slices oily reclining on the top or (iii) does not have condensed mushroom soup as a principal ingredient. None the less they seem inordinately enchanted by bubble and squeak for reasons they are unable to quite explain. They do not use silverware at all well too.

Bubble and Squeak was almost always

made with leftovers - particularly
mashed potatoes and vegetables and was
commonly consumed for breakfast with
bacon or sausage and a nice lightly
fried egg dribbling naughtily over it.

In days of yore left over vegetables
and meat was often an ingredient as
appeared in Mrs. Maria Eliza Ketelby
Rundell's seminal and well-fingered
tome *New System of Domestic Cookery:
Founded upon Principles of Economy;
and Adapted to the Use of Private
Families* (1806).

Ms. Rundell wrote: "Boil, chop, and
fry, with a little butter, pepper, and
salt, some cabbage, and lay on it
slices of rare done beef, lightly
fried"

Bubble and Squeak was very popular

during World War II when meat was scarce and only knobs could get rare done beef.

Bubble and Squeak is so called, it seems, because of the attractive noises it makes whilst frying in skillet.

The Irish have a somewhat similar creation called Colcannon (most often cooked with kale) as do the Scots who have the enchantingly styled Rumbledethumps (most often made with mashed turnips in which the Scots are obviously kilt deep).

## Ingredients

4 tablespoons of best salted butter
½ cup of white or red onion, finely

chopped

Massive pile of left over lumpy mashed potato (whisking potato is for prison inmates only)

Any leftover vegetables, cabbage, swede, carrots, peas, Brussels sprouts, all quite finely chopped

Salt and freshly ground black pepper

## Preparation method

1. In a large frying pan melt the knob of best butter, add the chopped onion and fry gently for 3 minutes or until quite nicely soft (be careful not to burn onions but rather sweat them like a whore in church.

2. Turn the heat up slightly and add the great pile of leftover mashed potato and vegetables. Fry for 10 minutes turning over in the melted butter now and again ensuring the

potato and vegetables are thoroughly reheated plus you are aiming to brown the outside edges to a sensuous golden color but not to burn the bubble and squeak. Press the potato mixture on to the base of the pan with a spatula and leave to cook gently for 1 min. Flip over and repeat until you have a lovely golden crispy all-over effect.

4. Bubble and squeak also makes a spectacular luncheon dish with a fried egg on top or it can of course be served with the rest of the iconic Full English breakfast (see *post*).

Americans are not at all comfortable with food that is not (i) served on a stick (ii) has non-dairy processed American cheese slices oily reclining on its top or (iii) has condensed mushroom soup as a principal ingredient. None the less they seem enchanted by bubble and squeak for reasons they are presently unable to explain.

Bubble and Squeak was almost always made with leftovers particularly mashed potatoes and vegetables and was commonly consumed for breakfast with bacon or sausage and a nice lightly fried egg dribbling naughtily over it. In days of yore left over vegetables and meat was often an ingredient as appeared in Mrs. Maria Eliza Ketelby Rundell's seminal and well fingered tome *New System of Domestic Cookery: Founded upon Principles of Economy; and Adapted to the Use of Private Families (1806)*.

The Irish have a somewhat similar creation called *Colcannon* (most often cooked with kale) as do the Scots who have *Rumbledethumps* (most often made with mashed turnips in which the Scots are obviously kilt deep).

## Ingredients

4 tablespoons of best salted butter
½ cup of white or red onion, finely chopped
 Massive pile of left over lumpy mashed potato (whisking potato is for prison inmates only)
 Any leftover vegetables, cabbage, swede, carrots, peas, Brussels sprouts, all quite finely chopped
 Salt and freshly ground black pepper

## Preparation Method

1.  In a large frying pan melt the knob of best butter, add the chopped onion and fry gently for 3 minutes or until quite nicely soft (be careful not to burn onions but rather sweat them like a whore in church.)

2. Turn the heat up slightly and add the great pile of leftover mashed potato and vegetables. Fry for 10 minutes turning over in the melted butter now and again ensuring the potato and vegetables are thoroughly reheated plus you are aiming to brown the outside edges to a sensuous golden color but not to burn the bubble and squeak.

Press the potato mixture on to the base of the pan with a spatula and leave to cook gently for 1 min. Flip over and repeat until you have a lovely golden all over effect.

4. Bubble and squeak also makes a spectacular lunch with a fried egg on top or can be served with the rest of the *Full English* breakfast.

## 5 FAGGOTS AND MUSHY PEAS

Knocking up a mess of faggots

There are lots of things about Britain that confuse Americans (including cricket where shouting does not help when attempting to describe the game) but even the suggestion of gobbling a couple of nice juicy fagots will send them into a state of near apoplexy.

Faggots are offal based meatballs made from pork hearts, liver, fatty belly meat, with herbs, breadcrumbs, and seasonings added.

They are cheap to make and the ingredients are readily available at most butchers except supermarkets which rarely keep offal.

Again, they were commonly eaten during World War II when prime cuts were eaten by the knobs. They are very nutritious with many trace elements. It is claimed "Faggots originated as a traditional cheap food of ordinary country people in Western England, particularly west Wiltshire and the West Midlands. Their popularity spread from there, especially to South Wales in the mid-nineteenth century, when many agricultural workers left the land to work in the rapidly expanding industry and mines of that area.

Faggots are also known as "ducks" or "savoury ducks" in some areas. The first recorded use of the appeared in the *Manchester Courier and Lancashire General Advertiser* of Saturday 3 June 1843, in which a news report of a gluttonous man who consumed twenty faggots.

Later, in 1851, a description of a

similar dish made from chopped liver and lungs in caul fat, the thin membrane surrounding the stomach, appeared.

## Ingredients

4 oz/110g fatty pork shoulder, roughly chopped

4 oz/ 110g pig's liver, roughly chopped

1 small red chili, de-seeded and finely chopped

Salt and Pepper

4 oz/110g bacon scraps

4 oz/ 110g bread crumbs

1 medium onion, finely chopped

1/2 tsp mace

1 tsp allspice

2 tbsp chopped parsley

2 sage leaves, finely chopped

8 oz/250g fatty belly pork, roughly

chopped

Large piece of Caul fat

## Preparation method

### Preheat the oven to 445°F

1. Mince all the roughly chopped meats in a handy-dandy hand mincer. If you do not have a mincer, then chop using a common or garden food processor but do take care not to over mix or you will create a mush, rather than a firm minced meat mix.

2. Place the minced meat into a large bowl. The, into the bowl, add the breadcrumbs, the onion, the herbs, spices and a pinch of salt and pepper. Mix thoroughly.

3. Moisten your hands under running cold water, then divide and roll the minced meat mixture into 8 nice plump evenly sized balls.

4. Wrap each of your balls in caul making sure the caul overlaps and is secure. This wrapping is the container for the faggot and needs to be strong. The caul will seal the faggots as they cook thus holding them together.

5. Place the faggots onto a baking sheet and bake in the hot oven for 50 - 60 minutes.

6. Once cooked, remove from the oven and serve immediately.

Serve with mushy peas, and lumpy mashed potatoes (see post).

A splendidly delicious plate of home-made faggots, mashed potatoes, and mushy peas. Delight your family by announcing proudly "It's high time we had a nice couple of faggots for dinner".

## 6 WELSH RAREBIT

There is no evidence that the Welsh actually originated Welsh rabbit (is it was originally styled), although they have always had a reputation for it together with male voice choirs, coal mining, rugby and sheep. It is reported  "a fourteenth-century text tells the tale that the Welsh people in heaven were being troublesome, and in order to get rid of them St Peter went outside the Pearly Gates and shouted 'Caws pobi' (Welsh for 'toasted cheese')—whereupon all the Welsh rushed out and the gates were shut on them)".

Rather like the offensive to some 'Chinese Fire Drill, Chinese Home-Run, and Chinese Puzzle" 'Welsh' in the seventeenth and eighteenth centuries was used as "a patronizingly humorous epithet for any inferior grade or variety of article, or for a substitute for the real thing."

It has been suggested Welsh rabbit may therefore have started life as a dish resorted to when meat was not available. The first record appears in

John Byron's Literary Remains (1725): "I did not eat of cold beef, but of Welsh rabbit and stewed cheese."

There are numerous decent regional and international variations of this tea-time favorite and the author remembers fondly his dear old mum making it when he finally arrived home from school having battled deep snow and packs of wolverines in walking the perilous seven miles while avoiding gangs of cut-throat brigands and the French, or so he mistily recalls.

A similar preparation to modern Welsh rarebits appears in good old Hannah Glasse (1747) who provides a simple recipe: 'To make a Scotch Rabbit. Toast a Piece of Bread, butter it, cut a Slice of Cheese, toast it on both sides, and lay it on the Bread'. The essential difference being the particular (Dunlop) cheese she lists. Rabbit was the original name but rarebit first appears in 1781.

Ever economical, the Frogs refer to it as Le Welsh.

Even the reclusive poor old Benn Gunn hankers for his toasted cheese in Robert Louis Stevenson's *Treasure Island* (1883) in which he gloomily bemoans, "Many's the long night I've dreamed of cheese —toasted".

## Ingredients

2 tablespoons salted best butter
2 tablespoons self-raising flour
1 tablespoon Coleman's magnificent mustard powder, or to taste
1/2 teaspoon cayenne pepper
3/4 cup strong Guinness (drink the

other quarter plus another full bottle or two)

2 tablespoons Worcestershire sauce

1 pound Cheddar, Double Gloucester or other semi-hard English cheese (avoid anything American if you can possibly avoid it.

4 to 8 pieces lightly toasted sourdough bread

## Preparation Method

1. Put butter in a saucepan over medium heat and, as it melts, stir in flour. Continue to cook; stirring occasionally and vigorously, until golden brown and enchantingly fragrant, 3 to 5 minutes or one quick beer should suffice.

Stir in Coleman's marvelous mustard powder and cayenne pepper, then whisk in Guinness and Worcestershire sauce.

2. When mixture is uniform, lower the heat and carefully stir in cheese until all nice and smooth. Carefully lift from heat and pour into a broad container

3. Spread the mixture thickly on toast and put under broiler all lovely and until bubbly and edges of toast are crisp. Serve immediately with a nice foaming pint of beer with your favorite recording of a Welsh Male Voice Choir echoing from distant Valleys. There's lovely look you!

## 7 STARGAZY PIE

Stargazy pie is a Cornish dish made principally from baked pilchards or nice plump, naughty sardines together with eggs and/or potatoes, covered with a golden brown pastry crust. The author's family has lived in Cornwall for generations. The author recalls a number of his old aunts who still spoke many words of Cornish. Sadly, all of these redoubtable old gentlewomen went quite mad living on the Bodmin Moors and other isolated places like Piper's Pool where she was briefly the only resident.

The Chapel, Pipers Pool, Cornwall by John Coupland

The author recalls that o n the first and third Sunday of each month at 11 am his Great Aunt Rose shared with herself an informal way of worship called 'Café Church'.

This was held in the school room where she enjoyed coffee, tea and nibbles whilst being guided through the session by a different leader (herself) each month.
She was also the Mayor and Postmistress.

Another Great Aunt the wonderfully odd Aunt Florence was likely completely bonkers and during WW I bicycled over the desolate Moors shouting "Kaiser Wilhelm is a bastard with a small willy, I know because I once saw it!"

Sadly in the late 1950s she was locked away in the appalling Bodmin Asylum, whose postcards belied the vileness of its grim and forbidding interior.

Bodmin Asylum

Stargazy Pie is a Cornish favorite around Christmas time.

The fish heads protruding through the crust seemingly gazing - skyward somewhat akin to the famous statue of the Roman Emperor Constantine - and the staring vacantly above gives this enigmatic crusty pie its enchanting name.

Stargazy Constantine

Apart from its stunning appearance, the oils released from the heads during cooking flow back into the pie making it both delightfully moist and flavorful.

The delightful fishing village of

Mousehole, it is claimed, is where the dish originated.

According to local folk-lore, "Prepared in the Ship Inn, ate on 23rd December- Tom Bawcock's Eve. Long ago winter storms had prevented the fishing boats putting to sea. In a lull in the bad weather, one of their number sterling Tom Bawcock managed to catch enough fish to prevent the village from starving. A pie of many fishes was made from the catch - Star Gazy Pie." A great story too!

## Ingredients for the pie crust

2 $1/4$ cups all-purpose flour, plus a little extra for sprinkling
1 tsp. kosher salt
1 tsp. Coleman's divine mustard powder
12 tbsp. Salted butter, chilled and

nicely cubed

6 tbsp. ice-cold water

## Ingredients for the pie filling

6 slices best bacon, cut into 1" bits

2 tbsp. salted butter

1 medium white or yellow onion, finely chopped

$1/2$ cup chicken stock

$1/3$ cup crème fraîche

2 tbsp. Coleman's divine powdered mustard

2 tbsp. finely chopped leaf parsley

1 tablespoon of fresh tarragon

1 tbsp. fresh Mayer lemon juice

2 nice brown fresh eggs, beaten

Kosher salt and freshly ground black peppercorns

8 fresh sardines, carefully

cleaned with their naughty heads
attached

3 nice brown eggs well hard-boiled,
peeled, and sliced (after cooking put
them in a Mason jar and shake them
vigorously - all the shells will come
off! Good for keeping garlic too!)

**Preparation method**

**Make the crust:**

1. Whisk flour, mustard, and salt
in a bowl. Using your fingers, cut
butter into flour mixture, forming
pea-size crumbles. Add water; work
dough until smooth but with
visible flecks of butter.

2. Divide the naughty dough in
half and flatten into disks. Wrap
the disks in plastic wrap; chill 1

hour before using.

## Make the filling

1. Heat bacon in a 4-qt. saucepan over a nice medium-high heat; cook until slightly crisp, 5-7 minutes.

2. Using a slotted spoon, transfer bacon to paper towels to drain. Add butter and onion to pan; cook until golden, 5-7 minutes. Remove from heat; whisk in the stock, crème fraîche, mustard, parsley, tarragon, lemon juice, half the egg, and Kosher or nun-blessed salt; set aside.

## Assemble and bake the stargazy pie:

1. Heat the oven to 400° F. On a lightly floured pastry board, roll 1 disk of the pie dough into a 12″ round

piece. Fit into a 9″ pie plate; carefully trim the edges, leaving about 1 1/2″ dough overhanging. Arrange the naughty little sardines in a clock-like pattern with their sad looking little heads resting along edge of crust.

3. Pour the filling over sardines; top with the reserved bacon, the nice hard-boiled eggs, salt, and pepper to taste.

4. Roll remaining disk of dough into a 12″ round; cut eight 1″ slits in dough about 2″ from the edge.

5. Place over the top of the pie and very gently pull sardine heads through slits. Pinch both the top and bottom edges together and fold under; crimp the edges.

6. Brush with remaining egg and cut three 1″-long slits in top of pie;

bake until crust is golden and filling is bubbling, 35-40 minutes.

7. Let cool slightly before serving.

8. Drink a lot of English beer or a bucket of fine French red win with the lovely, fishy, pie.

A man walks into a bar in Mousehole, Cornwall with a large stargazy pie on his head. The barman asks, "Why do you have a stargazy pie on your head?" The man replies "It's a family tradition."

## 8 JELLIED EELS

Freshwater eels were considered a cheap, yet delightful repast since they were once awfully plentiful in the now nastily polluted River Thames

They were most commonly obtained from Billingsgate Fish Market where very oddly and during the naughty 18$^{th}$ century, they were only sold there by Dutch eel fishermen whom, it transpires, were being rewarded for supplying the City of London with food immediately after the Great Fire of 1666.

Perhaps, and by dint of similar reasoning, Americans should only be permitted to sell their food to themselves.

Eels have particularly unusual mating habits that require them to travel for about six months at about 20 miles a day to the Sargasso Sea where they writhe about in a mass of fishy unseemliness. The adults die after spawning, and the young eels head back to freshwater. In captivity they can live to at least 85. If one were an eel, therefore, it might make more sense to stay at home in someone's tank.

It seems eel sex is nothing much to swim home about.

Eel meat is firm with a considerable

fat content, but has an excellent full-bodied flavour when cooked.

Uncooked flesh is unappetizingly grey of hue but becomes nicely light and flaky when cooked.

Since eels are naturally gelatinous, a jelly is formed when eels cool after cooking.

Extra jelly can be simply produced by adding gelatine (processed animal collagen) during the complicated cooking process.

This recipe will serve 4-6 people, one glutton, or one lady antique dealer.

## Ingredients

3 pounds fresh eel, peeled, cleaned and cut into 2-inch pieces

1/4 cup of Sarson's malt vinegar

1 medium-sized white onion, peeled and very thinly sliced

12 whole black peppercorns, wrapped in a cheesecloth packet and tied

2 small bay leaves

1/4 cup freshly squeezed lemon juice

2 tbsp of curly parsley, finely chopped

2 tsp. Kosher salt (blessed by a nun will do if no Rabbis are available)

2 1/2 cups water

2 hard-boiled brown free range eggs for garnish.

**Preparation method**

1. Wash the pieces of the three pounds of naughty eel thoroughly under cold running water while thinking of a suitable alibi.

2. Place the nicely cut pieces of eel in Kosher salted water (or nun blessed salted water) and let them soak therein for 5 minutes.

3. Rinse well under cold running water, then place the eel pieces in a heavy 4 - to 5-quart stainless-steel or enameled saucepan.

4. Add the Sarson's malt vinegar, peppercorns, bay leaves, finely sliced onion, Kosher or nun blessed salt and water, and bring to a vigorous rolling boil over high heat.

 Eel meat is firm with a considerable fat content but has

an excellent full-bodied flavour when cooked. Uncooked flesh is unappetizingly grey of hue but becomes nicely light and flaky when cooked. Since eels are naturally gelatinous, a jelly is formed when eels cool after cooking.

5. Extra jelly can be simply produced by adding gelatin (processed animal collagen) during the complicated cooking process.

6. Transfer the pieces of eel into a nice baking dish (8" x 12" x 2" inches would be perfect) with a slotted spoon, and stir the lemon juice into the cooking liquid. Fish out the peppercorns and discard them.

7. Pour the contents of the pan over the eel, spreading the onion slices on

top with a fork. Listen carefully since you may hear the eel groan slightly with pleasure at this point.

8. Pour into your favorite serving bowl and sprinkle nicely and evenly with the finely chopped curly parsley, and refrigerate for at least 4 hours. Drink several more Martinis while this takes place. When thoroughly chilled, the liquid should form a lovely sensuous soft jelly.

9. Cut eggs crosswise into 1/4-inch slices and arrange them attractively on the jelly and serve directly from the bowl.

This recipe will serve 4-6 people or one glutton

### How to Clean a Naughty Eel

Eel cleaning is not for the

pusillanimous and indeed both The Israeli Army and The French Foreign Legion require recruits to be able to clean an eel behind their backs while under mortar fire.

1. Firstly wash your eel thoroughly under cold water for about half an hour in England or two hours in France where clean water may not be readily available. Thereafter carefully and lovingly scrape your eel to remove any remaining traces of eel slime (still used by the Dutch in cosmetics).

2. Violently gut the well washed eels being particularly vigilant to slit the belly about an inch and a bit beyond the vents in order to remove the kidney.

3. Tenderly scrub the gut cavity and wash it out fastidiously to remove all

traces of blood from the backbone and throat, and then rinse the eel again.

4. Lie down for a while and drink two stiff Martinis. Your eel is now ready to jelly.

## 9  SCOTCH EGGS

The glorious Scotch egg, much beloved by The Brits and the author's daughter

Lydia, consists of nice gooey semi-hard boiled eggs reclining in an all-enveloping blanket of seasoned pork sausage meat and lightly dusted with breadcrumbs.

Coleman's delightful English mustard and a foaming pint of best English bitter is a lovely accompaniment.

Scotch eggs are probably Britain's favorite pub snack. The origins of the dish area still little uncertain. During the 18$^{th}$ and 19$^{th}$ centuries there was a large egg trade out of Scotland eggs when the merchants dipped eggs in boiling water and then left in  lime-powder disinfectant in a process called 'scotching' for transportation and also increased shelf-span. They were unattractively discolored and it is claimed that stuffing them in sausage meat avoided their repelling aspect and they were still quite edible. Further, the store Fortnum & Mason claims that in at least 1738 they sold the dish made with pullet eggs and gamier sausage meat similar to pâté.

There are other theories as in Mrs. Rundell's book *'A New System of Domestic Cookery'* in which scotched eggs were served hot with gravy and Nargisi Kofta, an Indian dish that is also made from minced meat and a boiled egg.

## Ingredients

6 almost hard-cooked nice local jumbo brown eggs, well chilled
1 pound of your favorite breakfast sausage or chorizo for daredevils

1/2 cup all-purpose flour

2 nice local brown jumbo eggs beaten

3/4 cup fine bread crumbs

Vegetable oil for frying

## Preparation method

1. Peel eggs and set aside (see Mason jar method ante).

2. Divide sausage into 6 portions. Roll each egg in flour and with finely manicured washed hands press a portion of the sausage around each egg.

3. Dip sausage-wrapped eggs into beaten eggs and roll in bread crumbs. Heat vegetable oil to 350 F.

4. Cook each egg in oil about 4-5

minutes or until sausage is cooked and browned. Drain on paper towel. Serve warm with lashings of Coleman's English mustard.

## 10 THE FULL ENGLISH

The full English is an English jewel craved by ex-patriots who have often thought about killing foreigners to get hold of it in all of its greasiness. The recipes will not be set out below since the author has been threatened by a group of elderly seaside bed-and-breakfast ladies with horrible retributions including having his privates stuffed into an old electric toaster set to 9.

However the contents of the plate itself were begrudgingly allowed. The dish is almost infinitely variable but the basic contents are set below.

1. Eggs (either fried or scrambled (runny fried eggs are by far the best).

2. Mushrooms freshly picked field mushrooms seem superior.

3. Grilled tomatoes.

4. Several rashers of best Danish bacon

5. A nice plump pork sausage.

6. Black or white pudding (sometimes called blood pudding).

7. A few sautéed new potatoes (nice and crispy) or  bubble and squeak

8. Baked beans

A nice pot of finest tea (not made with tea-bags) tomato ketchup, Worcester Sauce, ground white pepper, brown sauce, vinegar, and Coleman's English Mustard should be loitering expectantly nearby.

## Blood or Black Pudding

Blood pudding or black (also white) pudding is certainly not everyone's cup-of-tea.

Talented chefs have recently found ways to incorporate black pudding into salads and main dishes even though it is most often thought of as a breakfast ingredient. Black pudding recipes vary wildly, but oatmeal is the best traditional thickener.

Steel-cut or pinhead oatmeal is essential and avoids cooking until it gets all nasty and mushy. Cook it until just tender.

Individual bits of the oats should be visible in the final product.

If you have a butcher that can get you fresh pig's blood, you are up and running!

## Ingredients

4 cups fresh pig's blood

2 1/2 teaspoons Kosher or nun-
blessed salt

1 1/2 cups steel-cut oatmeal

2 cups very finely diced pork fat
finely chopped

1 large yellow or white onion,
finely chopped

1 cup whole milk

1 1/2 teaspoons freshly ground
black pepper

1 teaspoon well-ground allspice

**Preparation Method**

1. Preheat your immaculate oven to
325° F and well grease 2 glass loaf

pans. Stir 1 teaspoon of Kosher or nun-blessed salt into the blood.

2. Bring 2 1/2 cups water to a boil and stir in the oats. Simmer away, stirring from time to time, while you drink a nice cold beer. 15 minutes, until just tender.

3. Pour the blood through a fine sieve into a large bowl to remove any nasty lumps, fishing lures, bottle caps etc. Stir in the fat, yellow or white onion, whole milk, black pepper, allspice and remaining 1 1/2 teaspoons salt. Add the oatmeal and mix together very well. Divide the naughty mixture between the two pans, cover with foil, and bake for 1 hour, until

all lovely and firm. Cool completely. Seal in plastic wrap. It is tastiest if eaten immediately. It is best not to keep it hanging about.

4. To serve, cut a slice about 1/2-inch thick off the loaf. Fry in best butter or oil until the edges are crisped and browned.

Delightful!

## 11. ENGLISH CHRISTMAS DINNER

Rather like the Full-English, the British Christmas Dinner is a closely guarded secret so only the dishes themselves will be listed not how to make them. There is no doubt that before the Revolution an American Christmas dinner was likely delightful as in 1685 "A Bill of Fare for Christmas Day, and how to set the Meat in Order.: Oysters. 1. A collar of brawn. 2. Stewed Broth of Mutton marrow bones. 3. A grand Sallet. 4. A pottage of caponets. 5. A breast of veal in stoffado. 6. A boil'd partridge. 7. A chine of beef, or surloin roast. 8. Minced pies. 9. A Jegote of mutton with anchove sauce. 10. A made dish of sweet-bread. 11. A swan roast. 12. A pasty of venison. 13. A kid with a pudding in his belly. 14. A steak pie. 15. A haunch of venison roasted. 16. A turkey roast and stuck with cloves. 17. A made dish of chickens in puff paste. 18. Two bran geese roasted, one larded. 19. Two large capons, one larded. 20. A

Custard. And further; "The second course for the same Mess. Oranges and Lemons. 1. A Young lamb or kid. 2. Two couple of rabbits, two larded. 3. A pig souc't with tongues. 4. Three ducks, one larded. 5. Three pheasants, 1 larded. 6. A Swan Pye. 7. Three brace of partridge, three larded. 8. Made dish in puff paste. 9. Bolonia sausages, and anchovies, mushrooms, and Cavieat, and pickled oysters in a dish. 10. Six teels, three larded. 11. A Gammon of Westphalia Bacon. 12. Ten plovers, five larded. 13. A quince Pye, or warden pye. 14. Six woodcocks, 3 larded. 15. A standing Tart in puff-paste, preserved fruits, Pippins &c. 16. A dish of Larks. 17. Six dried neats tongues. 18. Sturgeon. 19. Powdered Geese. Jellies."

The reasons for this are complicated but include the following: The British do not make green bean casseroles, serve green jello, cook dry Turkey, or shoot family members at the table.

Even later in 1847 in *American System of Cookery*, by Mrs. T. J. Crowen we find "To Arrange a Christmas Dinner. Place a high pyramid of evergreens (made as before directed) in the centre of the table. Let a roasted turkey of uncommon size occupy the middle or centre of one side of the table, on one end let there be a cold boiled ham, and at the other, fricasseed chicken or a roast pig; with the turkey serve mashed potatoes and turnips, boiled onions and dressed celery, or other salad with apple sauce--near the ham place fried or mashed potatoes and pickles or mangoes: and with the pig or fricassee, the same as with the turkey; large pitchers of sweet cider (or where that is not desired, ice water) should be placed diagonally opposite each other, on two corners of the table; boiled turkey with oyster sauce may occupy the place of the fricassee, or instead, a fine oyster pie. For dessert, there should be only two very large and ornamental mince pies, one sufficiently large that each of the company may be helped from it, in token of common interest, is desirable. Ice creams and jellies and jams and ripe fruits and nuts, with sweet cider and syrup water of different sorts, or wines, complete the dessert. Biscuit and jelly sandwich may be served at dessert, or paste puffs and charlotte de russe or blancmange with strands of jelly."

And further:

"A Bill of Fare for Christmas Day, and how to set the Meat in Order.:
Oysters. 1. A collar of brawn. 2. Stewed Broth of Mutton marrow bones. 3. A grand Sallet. 4. A pottage of caponets. 5. A breast of veal in stoffado. 6. A boil'd partridge. 7. A chine of beef, or surloin roast. 8. Minced pies. 9. A Jegote of mutton with anchove sauce. 10. A made dish of sweet-bread. 11. A swan roast. 12. A pasty of venison. 13. A kid with a pudding in his belly. 14. A steak pie. 15. A hanch of venison roasted. 16. A turkey roast and stuck with cloves. 17. A made dish of chickens in puff paste. 18. Two bran geese roasted, one larded. 19. Two large capons, one

larded. 20. A Custard.

"The second course for the same Mess. Oranges and Lemons. 1. A Young lamb or kid. 2. Two couple of rabbits, two larded. 3. A pig souc't with tongues. 4. Three ducks, one larded. 5. Three pheasants, 1 larded. 6. A Swan Pye. 7. Three brace of partridge, three larded. 8. Made dish in puff paste. 9. Bolonia sausages, and anChoves, mushrooms, and Cavieate, and pickled oysters in a dish. 10. Six teels, three larded. 11. A Gammon of Westphalia Bacon. 12. Ten plovers, five larded. 13. A quince Pye, or warden pye. 14. Six woodcocks, 3 larded. 15. A standing Tart in puff-paste, preserved fruits, Pippins &c. 16. A dish of Larks. 17. Six dried neats tongues. 18. Sturgeon. 19.

Spotted Dick, Toad-in-the-Hole and Bubble and Squeak Powdered Geese. Jellies."

And finally things are still looking good in 1908 with "Problem of That Christmas Dinner: One Must Have Variety, So Here Are Four Ideas Which Don't Follow Tradition Too Closely," *New York Times*, December 20, 1908

"It is not so much the question this year what shall we have for our Christmas dinner as what shall we not have or rather what shall we dispense with to save expenses, as prices of food products are tremendous...we are Americans up to date and dominated largely by the 'New Thouts,' one of the principle of which is self-denial. So as Americans we will serve the best Christmas dinner we can afford and have enough for ourselves and our friends, without be in over extravagant. Besides a good dinner a little will be spent for Christmas greens and flower to decorate the table and the house...Here are four menus as suggestions for the Christmas dinner... **Menu No. 1.** Lynn Havens, Half Shell, Celery, Olives, Chicken Soup, Deviled Crabs En Coquille, Hothouse Cucumbers, Roast Sirloin or Prime Ribs of Beef, Seasoned Potatoes, Romaine Salad, Spinach, Roquefort Cheese, Toasted Biscuits and Wafers, Plum Pudding, Brandy Sauce, Ice Cream, Fruit, Nuts, and Raisins, Coffee.

**Menu No. 2.** Grape Fruit, Green Turtle Soup Clear, Radishes, Sliced Tomatoes, Boiled Striped Bass, Sauce Hollandaise, Bermuda Potatoes, Roast Saddle of Canada Mutton, Currant Jelly, Jerusalem Artichokes, Cream Sauce, Stuffed Green Peppers,

Spotted Dick, Toad-in-the-Hole and Bubble and Squeak
Pineapple Punch, Broiled Squab, Lettuce Salad, Celery and Stilton Cheese, Biscuit Tortoni, Fruit, Nuts, Rasisins, Coffee.

**Menu No. 3.** Cream of Oysters, Olives, Salted Pecans, Crab flakes au Gratin, Roast Turkey, Cranberry Jelly, Country Sausages, Mashed Potatoes, Boiled Onions, Celery Salad, Toasted Wafers, Edam Cheese, Deep Dish Apple Pie, Ice Cream, and Coffee.

**Menu No. 4.** Iced Oranges, Cream of Celery, Roast Goose, Apple Sauce, Mashed Potatoes, Fresh String Beans, Grape Fruit, Salad, Neuchatel Cheese, Toasted Wafers, Cream Tapioca Pudding, Plum Jelly, and Coffee.

In 2016 all is clearly over at Christmas with, dry turkey, canned gravy, instant mashed potatoes, dollar store stuffing, canned peas, green jello, spam, a stabbing, and a surprise visit from unexpected SWAT guests.

## An English Christmas dinner will likely consist

1. Smoked Scottish Salmon
2. Pate
3. Roast Chicken
4. Roast Goose or pheasant
5. Glazed Baked Ham
6. Brussels' Sprouts with Bacon
7. Sage and Onion Stuffing
8. Roasted Parsnips, Potatoes
9. Bread Sauce
10. Parsley Sauce
11. Cranberry Sauce
12. Gravy with White Port
13. Christmas Pudding with Rum Butter
14. Christmas Cake

Bon appetit!

The author's roasted pheasant

## ABOUT THE AUTHOR

Having spent most of his childhood as an idiot the author became a simpleton in middle-age and graduated to the lofty height of imbecile in 2011. He has been a cretin and noted curmudgeon for the last three years and eats twigs and chews crayons.

His one hundred and fifty-nine non best-sellers include Aglets through the Ages; All about the Naughty Little Things on the Ends of Shoelaces, Boiling Eggs for Simpletons, and The Lead in Your Pencil; A Concise History of Pencil Hardness. Dr. Pepperell has been a TV historian, a professional touring comedian and an octopus catcher in the Greek Islands. He is currently as mad as a cut snake.